Beginners I Cookbook & Guide

Super Simple and Delicious Homemade Pasta Recipes

BY

MOLLY MILLS

Copyright © 2019 by Molly Mills

License Notes

No part of this book may be copied, replicated, distributed, sold or shared without the express and written consent of the Author.

The ideas expressed in the book are for entertainment purposes. The Reader assumes all risk when following any guidelines and the Author accepts no responsibility if damages occur due to actions taken by the Reader.

An Amazing Offer for Buying My Book!

Thank you very much for purchasing my books! As a token of my appreciation, I would like to extend an amazing offer to you! When you have subscribed with your e-mail address, you will have the opportunity to get free and discounted e-books that will show up in your inbox daily. You will also receive reminders before an offer expires so you never miss out. With just little effort on your part, you will have access to the newest and most informative books at your fingertips. This is all part of the VIP treatment when you subscribe below.

SIGN ME UP: *https://molly.gr8.com*

Table of Contents

Delicious Homemade Pasta Recipes 7

Recipe 1: Easy Garlic Penne 8

Recipe 2: Simple One Pot Pasta 10

Recipe 3: Simple Pasta Carbonara 12

Recipe 4: Healthy Artichoke Pasta Salad 14

Recipe 5: Hearty Basil Spiced Chicken Over Angel Hair 16

Recipe 6: Summer Time Cucumber Pasta 19

Recipe 7: Tasty Asparagus and Ham Fettuccine 22

Recipe 8: Healthy Spaghetti Smothered in Mushrooms and Broccoli 24

Recipe 9: Delicious Smoked Salmon Tortellini Smothered in Bechamel Sauce 27

Recipe 10: Healthy Seafood Pasta Salad 31

Recipe 11: Creamless Primavera 33

Recipe 12: Linguine Smothered in Clams and Mushrooms 37

Recipe 13: Smother Rigatoni in Vodka Sauce 40

Recipe 14: Traditional Sausage Gnocchi 42

Recipe 15: Smooth Mint Pasta 46

Recipe 16: Easy Tomato Brie Pasta 48

Recipe 17: Healthy Chicken Pasta Salad 50

Recipe 18: Vegetarian Style Baked Pasta 53

Recipe 19: Tropical Style Shrimp Scampi 56

Recipe 20: Traditional Orzo Alfredo 59

Recipe 21: Spaghetti Smothered in Peanut Butter Sauce 61

Recipe 22: Chickpea Style Macaroni Salad 63

Recipe 23: Classic Arugula Pesto Smothered Pasta 66

Recipe 24: Classic Chicken Margherita 68

Recipe 25: Pasta Smothered in Tequila Spiced Tomato Sauce 70

About the Author 73

Don't Miss Out! 75

Delicious Homemade Pasta Recipes

AAAAAAAAAAAAAAAAAAAAAAAAAAAAAAAAAAAAAAAAAAAAAAAAAA

Recipe 1: Easy Garlic Penne

This is a simple pasta recipe that you can make when you don't have too much time to prepare a home cooked meal for yourself.

Yield: 4 Servings

Cooking Time: 20 Minutes

List of Ingredients:

- 1 Pack of Penne Pasta, Uncooked
- ¼ Cup of Olive Oil, Extra Virgin Variety and Evenly Divided
- 3 Cloves of Garlic, Finely Chopped
- 2 Tomatoes, Sun Dried Variety and Finely Chopped
- 1 tablespoon of Parsley, Dried
- 1 teaspoon of Red Pepper Flakes, Crushed
- ½ teaspoons of Black Pepper, For Taste
- ¼ Cup of Parmesan Cheese, Finely Grated

AAAAAAAAAAAAAAAAAAAAAAAAAAAAAAAAAAAAAAAAAAAAAAAAAAAA

Instructions:

1. The first thing that you will want to do is cook your pasta. To do this bring a large sized pot of water to a boil over high heat. Once the water is boiling add in your pasta and cook until tender. Once tender, drain and set aside for later use.

2. While your pasta is cooking heat up your oil in a large sized skillet placed over medium heat. Once the oil is hot enough add in your next 3 ingredients for at least one minute.

3. Season with your pepper flakes and pepper and stir to combine.

4. Add in your cooked pasta and remaining oil. Toss thoroughly to combine.

5. Remove from heat and serve topped with parmesan cheese.

Recipe 2: Simple One Pot Pasta

Just as the name implies this dish allows you to cook a full meal without having to use too many dishes in the process. This particular dish is incredibly delicious and makes for the perfect meal when you are running tight on time.

Yield: 6 Servings

Cooking Time: 30 Minutes

List of Ingredients:

- 1 teaspoon of Olive Oil, Extra Virgin Variety
- ½ Cup of Onion, Finely Sliced
- 1 Cup of Mushrooms, Fresh and Finely Sliced
- 1 Can of Tomatoes, Finely Diced
- 1 Cup of Water, Warm
- 2 teaspoons of Basil, Dried
- 1 teaspoon of Oregano, Dried
- 1 teaspoon of Sugar, White in Color
- ¼ teaspoons of Garlic, Powdered
- ¼ teaspoons of Black Pepper, For Taste
- 8 Ounces of Macaroni, Uncooked

Instructions:

1. First spray a large sized skillet with a generous amount of cooking spray.

2. Then add in your oil and heat over medium heat. Once hot enough add in your mushrooms and onions and continue to cook until tender. This should take at least 5 minutes.

3. Next add in your remaining ingredients except for your pasta. Stir thoroughly to combine.

4. Once your mixture begins to boil add in your pasta and cover.

5. Continue to cook for the next 20 minutes over low heat until your pasta is tender to the touch. Make sure that you stir your mixture every once in a while.

6. After this time remove from heat and serve whenever you are ready.

Recipe 3: Simple Pasta Carbonara

If you are looking for a simple and tasty meal, then this is the perfect recipe for you. It is so delicious I guarantee that you won't be able to just have one plate.

Yield: 2 Servings

Cooking Time: 20 Minutes

List of Ingredients:

- 1 Pack of Angel Hair Pasta, Uncooked
- 1 Onion, Medium in Size and Thinly Sliced
- ¼ Cup of Oil, Vegetable Variety
- 1 Cup of Ham, Fully Cooked and Cut Into Cubes
- ½ Cup of Chicken Broth, Homemade Preferable
- ¼ Cup of Margarine, Fully Melted
- 2 Egg Yolks, Beaten Thoroughly
- ½ Cup of Parsley, Fresh and Minced
- ½ Cup of Parmesan Cheese, Freshly Grated

AAAAAAAAAAAAAAAAAAAAAAAAAAAAAAAAAAAAAAAAAAAAAAAAAAAA

Instructions:

1. The first thing that you will want to do is cook your pasta. To do this bring a large sized pot of water to a boil over high heat. Once the water is boiling add in your pasta and cook until tender. Once tender, drain and set aside for later use.

2. While your pasta is cooking use a large sized skillet placed over medium heat and cook your onion in some oil until tender to the touch.

3. Then add in your next 3 ingredients and continue to cook until completely heated through.

4. Once your pasta is cooked add it to your ham mixture and toss thoroughly to coat.

5. Add in your remaining ingredients except for your cheese and toss again to combine.

6. Serve your pasta and top with your grated parmesan cheese. Enjoy while still piping hot.

Recipe 4: Healthy Artichoke Pasta Salad

Here is yet another great tasting pasta salad that is a perfect dish to make when you are looking for a healthy dish to enjoy. It is extremely tasty and surprisingly filling.

Yield: 2 Servings

Cooking Time: 4 Hours and 10 Minutes

List of Ingredients:

- 1 Cup of Macaroni, Salad Variety and Uncooked
- 1 Jar of Artichoke Hearts, Marinated
- ½ Cup of Mushrooms, Cut into Quarters
- 1 Cup of Tomatoes, Cherry Variety and Cut into Halves
- 1 Cup of Black Olives, Pitted
- 1 tablespoon of Parsley, Fresh and Roughly Chopped
- ½ teaspoons of Basil, Dried
- ½ Tablespoons of Oregano, Dried
- 2 Cloves of Garlic, Minced
- Dash of Salt and Pepper, For Taste

Instructions:

1. The first thing that you will want to do is cook your pasta. To do this bring a large sized pot of water to a boil over high heat. Once the water is boiling add in your pasta and cook until tender. Once tender, drain and set aside for later use.

2. While your pasta is cooking use a large sized mixing bowl and combine your remaining ingredients together until thoroughly combined.

3. Place this mixture and your cooked pasta into your fridge to chill for the next 4 hours.

4. Before you are ready to serve toss both your pasta and mixture together until thoroughly combined.

Recipe 5: Hearty Basil Spiced Chicken Over Angel Hair

This is a simple pasta recipe that you can make, but it is also incredibly delicious. This is the perfect recipes to put together when you are looking to make something a little more of the classy side.

Yield: 2 Servings

Cooking Time: 30 Minutes

List of Ingredients:

- 1 Pack of Angel Hair Pasta, Uncooked
- 2 teaspoons of Olive Oil, Extra Virgin Variety
- ½ Cup of Onion, Finely Chopped
- 1 Clove of Garlic, Finely Chopped
- 2 ½ Cups of Tomatoes, Finely Sliced
- 2 Cups of Chicken Breasts, Boneless, Skinless and Finely Chopped
- ¼ Cup of Basil, Fresh and Dried
- ½ teaspoons of Salt, For Taste
- 1/8 teaspoons of Hot Pepper, Sauce
- ¼ Cup of Parmesan Cheese, Finely Grated

AAAAAAAAAAAAAAAAAAAAAAAAAAAAAAAAAAAAAAAAAAAAAAAAAAAA

Instructions:

1. The first thing that you will want to do is cook your pasta. To do this bring a large sized pot of water to a boil over high heat. Once the water is boiling add in your pasta and cook until tender. Once tender, drain and set aside for later use.

2. While your pasta is cooking use a large sized skillet and place over medium to high heat. Add in your oil and once your oil is hot enough add in your remaining ingredients except for your parmesan cheese.

3. Allow your mixture to come to a boil before reducing the heat to a simmer. Allow to simmer for at least 5 to 10 minutes or until all of your veggies are soft.

4. Add in your cooked pasta and toss thoroughly to coat.

5. Remove from heat and serve with a garnish of Parmesan Cheese. Enjoy whenever you are ready.

Recipe 6: Summer Time Cucumber Pasta

Just as the name implies this is a great tasting pasta dish to make during the hot summer time months. It is light and filling, making it perfect for those who still wish to fit in their tiny bikinis.

Yield: 2 Servings

Cooking Time: 3 to 4 Hours and 15 Minutes

List of Ingredients:

- 8 Ounces of Pasta, Tube Variety and Uncooked
- 1 tablespoon of Oil, Vegetable Variety
- 2 Cucumbers, Fresh, Medium in Size and Thinly Sliced
- 1 Onion, Medium in Size and Thinly Sliced
- 1 ½ Cups of Sugar, White
- 1 Cup of Water, Warm
- ¾ Cup of Vinegar, White in Color
- 1 tablespoon of Mustard, Prepared Variety
- 1 tablespoon of Parsley Flakes, Dried
- 1 teaspoon of Salt, For Taste
- 1 teaspoon of Pepper, For Taste
- ½ teaspoons of Garlic, Salt Variety

AAAAAAAAAAAAAAAAAAAAAAAAAAAAAAAAAAAAAAAAAAAAAAAAAAAAA

Instructions:

1. The first thing that you will want to do is cook your pasta. To do this bring a large sized pot of water to a boil over high heat. Once the water is boiling add in your pasta and cook until tender. Once tender, drain and set aside for later use.

2. Once your pasta has slightly cooled, place into a large sized bowl along with your cucumbers and onions. Toss to thoroughly combine.

3. Add in your remaining ingredients and toss again to thoroughly coat.

4. Cover and place into your fridge to chill for the next 3 to 4 hours.

5. After this time serve whenever you are ready. Enjoy!

Recipe 7: Tasty Asparagus and Ham Fettuccine

This is a perfect pasta recipe for those who are looking for something a little more on the healthier side but that is still just as filling.

Yield: 4 Servings

Cooking Time: 25 Minutes

List of Ingredients:

- 12 Ounces of Fettuccini, Dry and Uncooked
- 8 Ounces of Asparagus, Fresh and Trimmed
- ½ Cup of Butter, Soft
- 2 Cups of Heavy Cream
- ¾ Cup of Parmesan Cheese, Finely Grated
- ¼ teaspoons of Garlic, Powdered Variety
- ¼ teaspoons of Black Pepper, For Taste
- Dash of Cayenne Pepper, For Taste
- ½ Pound of Ham, Fully Cooked and Finely Diced

AAAAAAAAAAAAAAAAAAAAAAAAAAAAAAAAAAAAAAAAAAAAAAAAAAAA

Instructions:

1. The first thing that you will want to do is cook your pasta. To do this bring a large sized pot of water to a boil over high heat. Once the water is boiling add in your pasta and cook until tender. Once tender, drain and set aside for later use.

2. Then add your asparagus to your pot and cook for another 5 minutes before draining.

3. While your pasta is cooking, heat up your heavy cream and butter in a medium sized saucepan placed over medium heat.

4. The moment your mixture begins to bubble, stir in your remaining ingredients and continue to cook until your mixture becomes thick in consistency.

5. Add in your cooked pasta and toss thoroughly to combine.

6. Serve while still piping hot and enjoy!

Recipe 8: Healthy Spaghetti Smothered in Mushrooms and Broccoli

This is a great pasta dish to make for those who are currently on a diet. This dish is low on the calories and still incredibly filling.

Yield: 4 Servings

Cooking Time: 35 Minutes

List of Ingredients:

- 1 Pound of Spaghetti, Uncooked
- 2 Packs of Broccoli, Frozen and Finely Chopped
- 2 Cans of Mushrooms, Finely Sliced and Drained
- ½ Cup of Butter, Soft
- 1 tablespoon of Salt, For Taste
- 2 teaspoons of Black Pepper, For Taste
- 1 Cup of Parmesan Cheese, Freshly Grated
- 2 teaspoons of Lemon Juice, Fresh
- 1 teaspoon of Garlic, Powdered Variety
- 1 teaspoon of Basil, Dried

AAAAAAAAAAAAAAAAAAAAAAAAAAAAAAAAAAAAAAAAAAAAAAAAAAAA

Instructions:

1. The first thing that you will want to do is cook your pasta. To do this bring a large sized pot of water to a boil over high heat. Once the water is boiling add in your pasta and cook until tender. Once tender, drain and set aside for later use.

2. While your pasta is cooking combine your remaining ingredients into a large sized saucepan and place over low heat. Cook until your mushrooms and broccoli are hot to the touch. Make sure that you stir constantly while your mixture is cooking.

3. Next place your cooked spaghetti onto your serving dishes and top off with your broccoli mixture. Enjoy while still piping hot.

Recipe 9: Delicious Smoked Salmon Tortellini Smothered in Bechamel Sauce

If you are an avid fan of seafood, then this is one recipe that you need to try for yourself at least once. It is incredibly delicious and makes for a tasty meal for virtually any occasion.

Yield: 4 Servings

Cooking Time: 25 Minutes

List of Ingredients:

- 2 Packs of Tortellini, Cheese Variety
- 1 ¼ Cups of Milk, Whole
- ¼ of an Onion, Small in Size and Finely Diced
- 1 Bay Leaf, Fresh
- 2 Cloves, Whole
- Dash of Nutmeg, Ground
- ¼ Cup of Butter, Soft
- 1 Red Bell Pepper, Finely Chopped and Seeded
- ½ Pound of Asparagus, Fresh, Trimmed and Cut into Quarters
- 10 Mushrooms, Fresh and Finely Sliced
- 1 Pound of Salmon, Smoked and Finely Diced
- 2 Tablespoons of Flour, All Purpose Variety

AAAAAAAAAAAAAAAAAAAAAAAAAAAAAAAAAAAAAAAAAAAAAAAAAAAA

Instructions:

1. The first thing that you will want to do is cook your pasta. To do this bring a large sized pot of water to a boil over high heat. Once the water is boiling add in your pasta and cook until tender. Once tender, drain and set aside for later use.

2. Then use a medium sized saucepan and place it over low heat. Once hot enough add in your next 5 ingredients and allow to simmer for the next 15 minutes.

3. After this time remove from heat and discard your onions, bay leaf and whole cloves.

4. Next melt your butter in a large sized skillet placed over medium heat. Once your butter is fully melted and add in your pepper and asparagus. Cook for the next 3 minutes.

5. Then add in your mushrooms and continue to cook until tender to the touch.

6. Once your mushrooms are tender add in your smoked salmon and continue to cook until completely heated through.

7. Then melt your butter in a separate small sized saucepan. Once melted add in your flour and whisk thoroughly until smooth in consistency.

8. Add in your milk and stir into your skillet with your salmon mixture.

9. Mix with your cooked pasta and toss thoroughly to coat. Serve whenever you are ready.

Recipe 10: Healthy Seafood Pasta Salad

This is a great seafood this to serve for your hardcore seafood lover. It is an incredibly easy seafood dish to make and I know it is one that is going to become a favorite in your household.

Yield: 4 Servings

Cooking Time: 3 Hours and 15 Minutes

List of Ingredients:

- 1 Pack of Pasta Shells, Small in Size and Uncooked
- 4 Stalks of Celery, Finely Chopped
- 4 Onions, Green in Color and Finely Chopped
- ½ A Bottle of French Dressing, Your Favorite Brand
- ½ A Bottle of Thousand Island Dressing, Your Favorite Brand
- ½ Cup of Mayonnaise
- 2 Cans of Tuna, Packed in Water, Drained and Flaked
- 2 Cans of Shrimp, Tiny Variety and Drained

Instructions:

1. The first thing that you will want to do is cook your pasta. To do this bring a large sized pot of water to a boil over high heat. Once the water is boiling add in your pasta and cook until tender. Once tender, drain and set aside for later use.

2. Then use a large sized bowl and mix together your cooked pasta and your remaining ingredients. Stir well until thoroughly combined.

3. Cover and place into your fridge to chill for the next 3 hours. Serve whenever you are ready.

Recipe 11: Creamless Primavera

Primavera, regardless of how you make it is always a tasty treat to enjoy whenever you wish. This is an easy dish to make for a late night dinner meal.

Yield: 6 Servings

Cooking Time: 40 Minutes

List of Ingredients:

- 1 Pack of Penne Pasta, Uncooked
- 1 Squash, Yellow in Color and Finely Chopped
- 1 Zucchini, Fresh and Finely Chopped
- 1 Carrot, Fresh, Peeled and Cut Julienne Style
- ½ A Red Bell Pepper, Cut Julienne Style
- ½ Pint of Tomatoes, Grape Variety
- 1 Cup of Green Beans, Fresh, Trimmed and Chopped Finely
- 5 Spears of Asparagus, Trimmed and Chopped Finely
- ¼ Cup of Olive Oil, Extra Virgin Variety and Evenly Divided
- ¼ teaspoons of Salt, For Taste
- ¼ teaspoons of Black Pepper, For Taste
- ½ Tablespoons of Lemon Juice, Fresh
- 1 tablespoon of Italian Seasoning, Dried
- 1 tablespoon of Butter, Soft
- ¼ of an Onion, Yellow in Color, Large in Size and Sliced Thinly
- 2 Cloves of Garlic, Chopped Finely
- 2 teaspoons of Lemon Zest, Fresh
- 1/3 Cup of Basil, Fresh and Roughly Chopped

- 1/3 Cup of Parsley, Fresh and Roughly Chopped
- 3 Tablespoons of Vinegar, Balsamic Variety
- ½ Cup of Romano Cheese, Finely Grated

AAAAAAAAAAAAAAAAAAAAAAAAAAAAAAAAAAAAAAAAAAAAAAAA

Instructions:

1. The first thing that you will want to do is preheat your oven to 450 degrees. Then line a baking sheet with one sheet of aluminum foil.

2. Next cook your pasta. To do this bring a large sized pot of water to a boil over high heat. Once the water is boiling add in your pasta and cook until tender. Once tender, drain and set aside for later use.

3. Then use a medium sized bowl and combine your next 12 ingredients together until thoroughly combined.

4. Place your veggies onto your baking sheet and place into your oven to roast for the next 15 minutes or until your veggies are tender to the touch.

5. Then heat up your remaining oil and butter together in a large sized skillet. Once your oil and butter mixture is hot enough add in your onions and garlic. Cook over medium heat until tender to the touch.

6. Then mix in your cooked pasta followed by your remaining ingredients except for your Romano cheese. Toss to thoroughly combine.

7. Last toss in your roasted veggies and garnish with your Romano cheese. Serve whenever you are ready.

Recipe 12: Linguine Smothered in Clams and Mushrooms

This is a tasty and hearty meal that you are definitely going to want to enjoy more than once. It is a great dish to make when you need to feed a large group of seafood lovers.

Yield: 6 Servings

Cooking Time: 50 Minutes

List of Ingredients:

- 1 Ounce of Mushrooms, Dried and Porcini Variety
- ¼ Cup of Olive Oil, Extra Virgin Variety
- 10 Cloves of Garlic, Minced
- 1 teaspoon of Red Pepper Flakes, Dried
- 36 Clams, Fresh and Cleaned
- 2 Cups of White Wine, Dry and Your Favorite Kind
- 4 Tomatoes, Fresh and Cut into Cubes
- 3 Jars of Clam Juice, Fresh
- 1 ½ Cups of Parsley, Fresh and Roughly Chopped
- 1 Pack of Linguine Variety and Uncooked

Instructions:

1. The first thing that you are going to want to do is soak your mushrooms for at least 20 to 30 minutes in some cold water. After this time dry your mushrooms and coarsely chop them.

2. Then heat up your oil in a medium sized saucepan placed over medium heat. Once the oil is hot enough add in your chopped mushrooms, red pepper flakes and minced garlic. Stir thoroughly to combine. Continue to cook until your mixture is brown in color.

3. Next stir in your white wine and clams and continue to cook until your clams open of their own accord. Discard any clams that remain sealed.

4. Add in your remaining ingredients except for your pasta and cook for the next 15 minutes on a simmer until thick in consistency.

5. The next thing that you will want to do is cook your pasta. To do this bring a large sized pot of water to a boil over high heat. Once the water is boiling add in your pasta and cook until tender. Once tender, drain and set aside for later use.

6. Toss in your pasta and continue to cook until completely heated through. Remove from heat and serve whenever you are ready.

Recipe 13: Smother Rigatoni in Vodka Sauce

This is one of my favorite pasta dishes and once you get a taste of it for yourself, I know it will become one of your favorites as well.

Yield: 4 Servings

Cooking Time: 25 Minutes

List of Ingredients:

- 1 tablespoon of Olive Oil, Extra Virgin Variety
- 1 Onion, Medium in Size and Finely Chopped
- 1 Clove of Garlic, Finely Chopped
- ¼ Cup of Vodka, Your Favorite Kind
- 1 Jar of Tomato Sauce, Your Favorite Kind
- 1 Box of Rigatoni, Uncooked

AAAAAAAAAAAAAAAAAAAAAAAAAAAAAAAAAAAAAAAAAAAAAAAAA

Instructions:

1. The first thing that you will want to do is cook your pasta. To do this bring a large sized pot of water to a boil over high heat. Once the water is boiling add in your pasta and cook until tender. Once tender, drain and set aside for later use.

2. Next heat up your olive oil in a large sized saucepan and place it over medium to high heat. Once your oil is hot enough add in your onions and cook until tender to the touch.

3. Then add in your garlic and continue to cook for an additional 30 seconds.

4. Add in your vodka and cook for another minute.

5. Stir in your sauce and bring your mixture to a boil. Once your mixture is boiling reduce the heat to low and cook for another 4 minutes.

6. Serve your pasta and ladle your sauce over the pasta. Serve while still piping hot and enjoy.

Recipe 14: Traditional Sausage Gnocchi

This is a traditional Italian inspired dish that I know you are going to want to make over and over again. It is extremely rich is taste and packed full of delicious flavor. I know you won't be able to get enough of it.

Yield: 4 Servings

Cooking Time: 40 Minutes

List of Ingredients:

- 1 tablespoon of Olive Oil, Extra Virgin Variety
- 1 Pound of Sausage, Italian Style
- 1 tablespoon of Olive Oil, Extra Virgin Variety
- ½ Cup of Onion, Finely Chopped
- 1 tablespoon of Garlic, Minced
- 1 ½ teaspoons of Italian Seasoning, Dried
- 1 Can of Tomatoes, Crushed
- 2 Tablespoons of Water, Warm
- ¼ teaspoons of Salt, For Taste
- 1 teaspoon of Sugar, White
- 1 tablespoon of Italian Seasoning, Dried
- 1 Pack of Gnocchi, Fresh
- Some Parsley, Fresh and Roughly Chopped
- Dash of Romano Cheese, Freshly Grated

AAAAAAAAAAAAAAAAAAAAAAAAAAAAAAAAAAAAAAAAAAAAAAAAAAAA

Instructions:

1. First heat up your olive oil in a large sized skillet placed over medium heat. Once the oil is hot enough add in your sausage and cook until brown in color. This should take at least 5 minutes. Once fully cooked remove and place on a plate lined with paper towels to drain.

2. The heat up some more oil in another large sized saucepan. Once the oil is hot enough add in your onions and cook until your onions are soft.

3. Add in your garlic and Italian seasoning. Cook for another 2 minutes.

4. Next add in your next 5 ingredients and stir thoroughly to combine.

5. Bring your mixture to a boil. Once your mixture is boiling reduce the heat to low and allow your mixture to simmer for the next 20 minutes while covered.

6. The next thing that you will want to do is cook your gnocchi. To do this bring a large sized pot of water to a boil over high heat. Once the water is boiling add in your gnocchi and cook until tender. Once tender, drain and set aside for later use.

7. Then stir your sausage mixture and toss with your gnocchi until thoroughly coated.

8. Garnish with your parsley and romano cheese and serve while still piping hot. Enjoy.

Recipe 15: Smooth Mint Pasta

While mint pasta may seem far from appetizing, I promise that once you get a taste you will soon change your mind. This is the perfect dish to make during the holiday season to really get you in the holiday mood.

Yield: 4 Servings

Cooking Time: 15 Minutes

List of Ingredients:

- 1 Pack of Linguini Pasta, Uncooked
- 6 Tomatoes, Seeded and Finely Chopped
- 20 Basil, Fresh
- 10 Mint Leaves, Fresh
- 2 Cloves of Garlic, Minced
- ½ Cup of Pine Nuts
- 3 Tablespoons of Parmesan Cheese, Grated
- 2 Tablespoons of Ricotta Cheese, Low in Fat
- 1 ½ Tablespoons of Olive Oil, Extra Virgin Variety
- Dash of Salt and Pepper, For Taste

AAAAAAAAAAAAAAAAAAAAAAAAAAAAAAAAAAAAAAAAAAAAAAAAAA

Instructions:

1. The first thing that you will want to do is cook your pasta. To do this bring a large sized pot of water to a boil over high heat. Once the water is boiling add in your pasta and cook until tender. Once tender, drain and set aside for later use.

2. Then use a food processor and blend your remaining ingredients on the highest setting until smooth in consistency.

3. Next toss your sauce with your cooked pasta and serve whenever you are ready.

Recipe 16: Easy Tomato Brie Pasta

This dish is one of the classiest pasta recipes that you can make today. It is revered by many Italian cuisine enthusiasts today and is one of the best tasting dishes you will ever have the chance to enjoy.

Yield: 4 Servings

Cooking Time: 20 Minutes

List of Ingredients:

- 1 Pack of Pasta, Bow Tie Variety
- 2 Cans of Tomatoes, Italian Style and Finely Diced
- ½ Pound of Brie Cheese, Cut into Small Cubes
- 2 Tablespoons of Basil, Fresh and roughly Chopped

AAAAAAAAAAAAAAAAAAAAAAAAAAAAAAAAAAAAAAAAAAAAAAAAAAAA

Instructions:

1. The first thing that you will want to do is cook your pasta. To do this bring a large sized pot of water to a boil over high heat. Once the water is boiling add in your pasta and cook until tender. Once tender, drain and set aside for later use.

2. While your pasta is cooking use a large sized saucepan and heat up your tomatoes over medium to high heat.

3. Bring your mixture to a boil and add in your cheese.

4. At a boil reduce your mixture to low and stir thoroughly until your cheese is fully melted.

5. Toss in your cooked pasta until thoroughly coated. Remove from heat and serve with a garnish of basil. Enjoy whenever you are ready.

Recipe 17: Healthy Chicken Pasta Salad

If you are looking for a healthier and light meal to enjoy, this is the perfect dish for you to enjoy. It is easy to make and makes for a great light meal to enjoy any time that you wish.

Yield: 2 Servings

Cooking Time: 2 Hours

List of Ingredients:

- 1 Can of Chicken Broth, Homemade Preferable
- ½ Cup of Mayonnaise, Low in Fat
- ¼ Cup of Parmesan Cheese, Finely Grated
- 1 teaspoon of Dill Weed, Dried
- 3 Cups of Pasta, Corkscrew Variety and Fully Cooked
- 1 Cup of Tomatoes, Cherry Variety and Cut Into Halves
- 1 Cup of Peas, Fully Cooked
- ½ Cup of Mushrooms, Finely Sliced
- 1 Rec Onion, Small in Size and Finely Chopped
- 2 Cups of Chicken, Fully Cooked and Cut Into Cubes
- 2 Leaves of Lettuce, Roughly Torn

AAAAAAAAAAAAAAAAAAAAAAAAAAAAAAAAAAAAAAAAAAAAAAAAAA

Instructions:

1. The first thing that you are going to want to do is mix together your first 4 ingredients together until thoroughly combined.

2. Then add in your remaining ingredients except for your lettuce. Stir again thoroughly until combined.

3. Cover your mixture and place into your fridge to chill for the next 2 hours.

4. When you are ready serve your mixture on top of your lettuce leaves.

Recipe 18: Vegetarian Style Baked Pasta

This is a great pasta recipe to make for those who are not only vegan friendly, but for those that are vegetarian friendly as well.

Yield: 6 Servings

Cooking Time: 1 Hour

List of Ingredients:

- 1 Pound of Pasta, Penne Variety and Uncooked
- 2 Tablespoons of Olive Oil, Extra Virgin Variety
- 8 Ounces of Mushrooms, Portobello Variety and Chopped Finely
- 1 teaspoon of Basil, Dried
- 1 teaspoon of Oregano, Dried
- 2 Cloves of Garlic, Minced
- 1 Jar of Spaghetti Sauce, Your Favorite Kind
- 4 Cups of Mozzarella, Finely Shredded
- 8 Ounces of Gorgonzola Cheese, Crumbled

AAAAAAAAAAAAAAAAAAAAAAAAAAAAAAAAAAAAAAAAAAAAAAAAAAAA

Instructions:

1. The first thing that you will want to do is cook your pasta. To do this bring a large sized pot of water to a boil over high heat. Once the water is boiling add in your pasta and cook until tender. Once tender, drain and set aside for later use.

2. Next preheat your oven to 350 degrees. While your oven is heating up grease a medium sized baking dish with an adequate amount of cooking spray.

3. Then use a large sized skillet and heat your oil in it. Once the oil is hot enough add in your mushrooms and cook for the next 2 minutes.

4. Then add in your next 3 minutes and cook for an additional minute.

5. Add in your sauce and stir thoroughly to coat. Remove from heat.

6. Pour some of your sauce mixture into the bottom of your baking dish and top off with your cooked pasta. Top this layer with both your cheeses. Repeat layers until all of your ingredients have been used up, making sure to end with your cheeses.

7. Place into your oven to bake for the next 30 to 45 minutes or until your cheese is brown in color. Remove and allow to cool slightly before serving.

Recipe 19: Tropical Style Shrimp Scampi

If you are an avid fan of the classic dish Shrimp Scampi, then this is one sweet dish that I know you are going to fall in love with. It is a great dish to prepare if you need to satisfy a particularly strong sweet tooth.

Yield: 4 Servings

Cooking Time: 25 Minutes

List of Ingredients:

- 1 Pack of Linguine, Uncooked
- ½ Cup of Olive Oil, Extra Virgin Variety
- ½ Cup of Pineapple Juice, Fresh
- ½ Cup of Orange Juice, Pulp Free
- 5 teaspoons of Orange Zest, Fresh and Finely Grated
- 1 teaspoon of Salt, For Taste
- 1 teaspoon of Black Pepper, For Taste
- 5 Cloves of Garlic, Peeled and Minced
- 1 Pound of Shrimp, Medium in Size and Deveined
- 2 Tablespoons of Parsley, Fresh and Roughly Chopped
- 2 Tablespoons of Parmesan Cheese, Freshly Grated

AAAAAAAAAAAAAAAAAAAAAAAAAAAAAAAAAAAAAAAAAAAAAAAAAA

Instructions:

1. The first thing that you will want to do is cook your pasta. To do this bring a large sized pot of water to a boil over high heat. Once the water is boiling add in your pasta and cook until tender. Once tender, drain and set aside for later use.

2. While your pasta is cook use a blender and combine your next 8 ingredients into it. Blend on the highest setting until smooth in consistency.

3. Pour your freshly blended sauce into a large sized skillet and place over medium to high heat. Bring your sauce to a simmer and cook for the next 2 minutes.

4. Then add in your shrimp and parsley, stir to combine. Continue cooking until your shrimp are completely pink. This should take at least 5 minutes.

5. Next take your cooked pasta and place onto serving plates. Spoon your shrimp mixture and sauce over your pasta and garnish with cheese. Enjoy whenever you are ready.

Recipe 20: Traditional Orzo Alfredo

If you are a huge fan of alfredo sauce, then I know you are going to love this recipe. It is surprisingly easy to make and will leave you wanting to make it over and over again.

Yield: 4 Servings

Cooking Time: 20 Minutes

List of Ingredients:

- 2 ½ Cups of Pasta, Orzo Variety and Uncooked
- ¼ Cup of Butter, Unsalted Variety and Soft
- ¼ Cup of Heavy Cream
- ¼ Cup of Parmesan Cheese, Finely Grated
- Dash of Nutmeg, Ground
- 1 tablespoon of Chives, Fresh and Roughly Chopped

AAAAAAAAAAAAAAAAAAAAAAAAAAAAAAAAAAAAAAAAAAAAAAAAAAAA

Instructions:

1. The first thing that you will want to do is cook your pasta. To do this bring a large sized pot of water to a boil over high heat. Once the water is boiling add in your pasta and cook until tender. Once tender, drain and set aside for later use.

2. While your pasta is cooking toss your pasta with your remaining ingredients except for your cheese and chives.

3. Once mixed garnish your pasta with your chives and cheese and serve whenever you are ready.

Recipe 21: Spaghetti Smothered in Peanut Butter Sauce

If you are a huge fan of Thai inspired dishes, then I know this is one pasta dish you are going to want to make over and over again.

Yield: 4 Servings

Cooking Time: 20 Minutes

List of Ingredients:

- ½ Cup of Peanut Butter, Creamy Style
- 1/3 Cup of Water, Hot
- 1 tablespoon of Soy Sauce, Light and Your Favorite Kind
- 1 Clove of Garlic, Crushed
- 1/3 Cup of Heavy Cream, Whipping Variety
- 1 teaspoon of Oil, Sesame Variety
- Dash of Chili Sauce, For Taste
- 12 Ounces of Spaghetti, Uncooked
- 3 teaspoons of Cilantro, Fresh and Roughly Chopped

Instructions:

1. The first thing that you will want to do is cook your pasta. To do this bring a large sized pot of water to a boil over high heat. Once the water is boiling add in your pasta and cook until tender. Once tender, drain and set aside for later use.

2. Next place your peanut butter into a small sized bowl. Add in your hot water and stir thoroughly until smooth in consistency.

3. Then add in your next 5 ingredients and continue stirring until smooth in consistency. Set aside for later use.

4. Next place your drained pasta into a large sized bowl and toss together with your peanut sauce until evenly coated. Serve whenever you are ready and serve with a garnish of cilantro for the tastiest results.

Recipe 22: Chickpea Style Macaroni Salad

This is another great dish to make if you are looking for something that is a little on the healthier side to enjoy. It is easy to make and absolutely delicious. I guarantee that even the pickiest eaters are going to love this dish.

Yield: 4 Servings

Cooking Time: 50 Minutes

List of Ingredients:

- 1 Cup of Macaroni, Dried and Uncooked
- 1 Can of Chickpeas, Drained
- 4 Tomatoes, Finely Chopped
- 1 Onion, Finely Chopped
- 1 Clove of Garlic, Minced
- 6 Ounces of Feta Cheese, Crumbled
- 1 Cup of Black Olives, Pitted
- 1 teaspoon of Salt, For Taste
- ½ teaspoons of Black Pepper, For Taste
- ½ Cup of Olive Oil, Extra Virgin Variety
- ¼ Cup of Lemon Juice, Fresh

AAAAAAAAAAAAAAAAAAAAAAAAAAAAAAAAAAAAAAAAAAAAAAAAAAA

Instructions:

1. The first thing that you will want to do is cook your pasta. To do this bring a large sized pot of water to a boil over high heat. Once the water is boiling add in your pasta and cook until tender. Once tender, drain and set aside for later use.

2. While your pasta is cooking combine your remaining ingredients in a large sized bowl until thoroughly combined.

3. While your macaroni is finished cooking, mix with your mixture.

4. Then cover and place into your fridge to chill for the next 30 minutes.

5. After this time serve whenever you are ready.

Recipe 23: Classic Arugula Pesto Smothered Pasta

Here is yet another type of pasta that you want to make if you are looking for a healthy pasta dish to enjoy.

Yield: 2 Servings

Cooking Time: 20 Minutes

List of Ingredients:

- ¼ Cup of Walnuts, Finely Chopped
- 3 Cloves of Garlic, Minced
- 2 Cups of Arugula, Chopped Coarsely
- ¼ Cup of Basil, Fresh and Coarsely Chopped
- ½ Cup of Olive Oil, Extra Virgin Variety
- 1/3 Cup of Parmesan Cheese, Freshly Grated
- Dash of Salt, For Taste
- Dash of Cayenne Pepper, For Taste
- 1 Pack of Penne, Uncooked

Instructions:

1. The first thing that you will want to do is cook your pasta. To do this bring a large sized pot of water to a boil over high heat. Once the water is boiling add in your pasta and cook until tender. Once tender, drain and set aside for later use.

2. Next combine your first 4 ingredients into a food processor and blend until coarsely chopped.

3. Pour your olive oil into your mixture and blend again until smooth in consistency.

4. Pour your mixture into a medium sized bowl and add in your next 3 ingredients and stir until thoroughly combined.

5. Once your pasta has finished cooking add it to your pesto mixture and toss thoroughly to combine. Serve whenever you are ready.

Recipe 24: Classic Chicken Margherita

This is a classic pasta dish that you can make when you are looking to enjoy a classic and filling dish. It is easy to make and makes for a filling and tasty meal for the whole family to enjoy.

Yield: 4 Servings

Cooking Time: 20 Minutes

List of Ingredients:

- 4 Chicken Breasts, Boneless, Skinless and Cut Into Halves
- 1 tablespoon of Olive Oil, Extra Virgin Variety
- 4 Ounces of Mozzarella, Fresh and Finely Sliced
- 2 Tablespoons of Basil Leaves, Fresh and Roughly Chopped
- 2 Cups of Pasta Sauce, Your Favorite Kind
- Some Cooked Pasta, Your Favorite Kind

AAAAAAAAAAAAAAAAAAAAAAAAAAAAAAAAAAAAAAAAAAAAAAAAAA

Instructions:

1. First season your chicken as you desire. Then heat up some olive oil in a large sized skillet and cook your chicken until brown in color.

2. Then add your pasta sauce to your chicken and cook over low heat for the next 5 minutes or until your chicken is completely cooked through.

3. Top off with some cheese and continue to cook until your cheese is completely melted.

4. Garnish with some basil and add in your cooked pasta.

5. Toss to combine and serve while still piping hot.

Recipe 25: Pasta Smothered in Tequila Spiced Tomato Sauce

If you are a huge fan of Tequila, then I know you are going to fall in love with this recipe. Be careful not to use too much tequila as you do not want to become drunk off your meal as you are consuming it.

Yield: 3 Servings

Cooking Time: 25 Minutes

List of Ingredients:

- 1 tablespoon of Butter, Soft
- ½ of an Onion, Finely Chopped
- 2 Cloves of Garlic, Minced
- ½ Tablespoons of Jalapeno Pepper, Pickled Variety and Finely Chopped
- 1 Can of Tomatoes, Finely Diced and Undrained
- 1 ½ Tablespoons of Tequila
- ¼ Cup of Water, Warm
- 1 Bottle of Clam Juice, Fresh
- Dash of Red Pepper Flakes, Crushed
- ¼ Pound of Macaroni, Elbow Variety
- 1 Lime, Fresh and Juice Only

AAAAAAAAAAAAAAAAAAAAAAAAAAAAAAAAAAAAAAAAAAAAAAAA

Instructions:

1. First melt your butter in a large sized skillet placed over medium heat.

2. Once your butter is fully melted add in your next 3 ingredients and cook until your onions are soft and translucent.

3. Then add in your next 4 ingredients.

4. Bring your mixture to a boil before adding in your macaroni. Cover and allow to simmer until your pasta is tender to the touch. This should take about 10 minutes.

5. Once tender remove from heat and stir in your fresh lime juice. Serve while still piping hot. Enjoy.

About the Author

Molly Mills always knew she wanted to feed people delicious food for a living. Being the oldest child with three younger brothers, Molly learned to prepare meals at an early age to help out her busy parents. She just seemed to know what spice went with which meat and how to make sauces that would dress up the blandest of pastas. Her creativity in the kitchen was a blessing to a family where money was tight and making new meals every day was a challenge.

Molly was also a gifted athlete as well as chef and secured a Lacrosse scholarship to Syracuse University. This was a blessing to her family as she was the first to go to college and at little cost to her parents. She took full advantage of her college education and earned a business degree. When she graduated, she joined her culinary skills and business acumen into a successful catering business. She wrote her first e-book after a customer asked if she could pay for several of her recipes. This sparked the entrepreneurial spirit in Mills and she thought if one person wanted them, then why not share the recipes with the world!

Molly lives near her family's home with her husband and three children and still cooks for her family every chance she gets. She plays Lacrosse with a local team made up of her old teammates from college and there are always some tasty nibbles on the ready after each game.

Don't Miss Out!

Scan the QR-Code below and you can sign up to receive emails whenever Molly Mills publishes a new book. There's no charge and no obligation.

Sign Me Up

https://molly.gr8.com

Printed in Great Britain
by Amazon